London

People, Parks and Places

Published in 2006 by
Binea Press, Inc.
512-1673 Richmond Street
London, Ontario, Canada N6G 2N3

Tel: 519.660.6424
Fax: 519.660.4449

E-mail: bineapress@bellnet.ca
www.bineapress.com

Distributed by:

Binea Press Inc.
519.660.6424

Library and Archives Canada Cataloguing in Publication

Bain, Richard (Richard G.), 1954-

London; People Parks and Places / Richard Bain

Foreword by Victor Garber

ISBN 0-9736863-6-7

1. London (Ont.)—Pictorial works.   I. Title.

FC3099.L65B335 2006   971.3'2600222   C2006-905131-3

Design by Response Generators
London, Ontario, Canada
Tel: 519.432.4932
www.rgdirect.com

Printed in Canada by Friesens Corporation
Altona, Manitoba

London

PEOPLE, PARKS AND PLACES

RICHARD BAIN

FOREWORD BY
VICTOR GARBER

For
Caroline, Daniel, Brett and Jordan

FOREWORD

When I come home to London and marvel at the growth and the changes, invariably my mind is filled with memories. Near the city's heart, and definitely at the center of mine, is the Grand Theatre, once my sanctuary. During my formative years, I would travel there on Saturday mornings to attend Children's Theatre classes to spend a few hours in another world; exploring my imagination.

Any doubts I may have had about myself, and "fitting in", would dissipate, absorbed into the worn walls of the second floor overlooking Richmond Street. The Artistic Director at the time, Peter Dearing and his charismatic wife Robin, were my first introduction to what I came to know as "theatre people". I can honestly say that my desire and love of performing started in those rooms, within those worn walls.

My family lived on Victoria Street in North London and I was only two blocks from Ryerson Public School where my siblings and I started our education. My first role was Santa Claus, in grade two I believe. I was not to be dissuaded by anyone and by the time I played Tom Sawyer at the Grand, I was well on my way.

My grandmother owned a bridal shop downtown on Dundas Street, where I would spend hours playing in the back of the store with my cousin Vicki. We would pretend that we were running the office, with great expertise. One of the benefits we shared was the enviable view of the Christmas parade from the upstairs window overlooking Dundas Street. It seemed to be such a thriving area in the early 60's, full of possibilities and potential. My father had a ladies store in London East, which seemed a world away from my Grandmother's place.

In those days, Commissioners Road seemed to be in the country. That's where my mother did her daily television show, "At Home With Hope Garber" on CFPL TV. It was a place that I loved to visit. The drive down the rural road led to this fortress where the magic of television was created and my mother was a pioneer in this medium. She interviewed celebrities and introduced fashion and cooking segments along with painting and flower arranging. She provided glamour and

A colourful autumn day
in Springbank Park.

intelligence on a daily basis and occasionally a song to top it off. Singing was always her first love. Today, when I go back and look at Central Collegiate, my high school, the beauty of the surroundings strikes me. The residences lining Waterloo Street are still impressive and the proximity to Victoria Park, which I was forced to circle repeatedly in gym class, provides an idyllic setting for teenage angst and optimism. I had plenty of both, and although my Central days were less than stellar, I can look back and appreciate the aesthetics of this area.

I would often walk from the Grand, where I would hang out, skipping morning classes… and stop at the London Café on Dundas for a plate of chips and gravy. Nothing however, could compare to the homemade chocolate doughnuts made fresh everyday at the old Covent Garden market. Yes the fruits and vegetables were impressive, but the doughnuts… I can still taste them.

Sundays at home on Victoria Street are something I remember with affection. Don Fleckser, who taught children's theatre at the Grand, would often come for the day. He would play original Broadway cast albums and talk about his trips to New York where he had seen some of these shows. I would bask in the afterglow of these visits, putting together the impossible plan for my Broadway debut, but with Don's inspiration, anything seemed possible!

Today, when I return to London to visit my brother and other family who still call this great city home, I am struck by its understated elegance and charm. I love walking with my sister-in-law, and their dog Sonny, through the seemingly unchanged paths of Gibbon's Park. Although London has obviously grown and spread considerably since I lived there, as Richard Bain's photographs depict, I am still aware of a peaceful city with a wonderful historic core at its heart.

I feel so very fortunate to have come from such a place.

Victor Garber

SPRINGTIME IN VICTORIA PARK WITH
THE CHANTICLEER PEAR TREES IN BLOOM.

*The Grand Theatre acts as a focal point
for London, a place where community
members can come together for inspiration,
entertainment and the opportunity
to socialize and network. Having this
beautiful, century-old theatre in London
instills a sense of pride, and positions our city
on an equal footing culturally and creatively
with other major centres in this country.*

*Deb Harvey
Executive Director, The Grand Theatre*

THE GRAND THEATRE,
BUILT IN 1901, FEATURING A UNIQUE
HAND-PAINTED PROSCENIUM ARCH,
HAS OFTEN BEEN DESCRIBED AS
CANADA'S "MOST BEAUTIFUL THEATRE".

MUSEUM LONDON, SITUATED AT THE "FORKS OF THE THAMES",
FEATURES THE WORKS OF MANY CONTEMPORARY AND
HISTORICAL ARTISTS INCLUDING JACK CHAMBERS,
GREG CURNOE AND PAUL PEEL.

ABOVE: RICHMOND AT DUFFERIN NEAR THE CITY'S CORE
IS HOME TO SOME GREAT RESTAURANTS AS WELL AS
ST. PETER'S CATHEDRAL BASILICA.

LEFT: ENJOYING SOME QUIET TIME
IN THE FOYER OF SOMERVILLE HOUSE ON THE CAMPUS OF
THE UNIVERSITY OF WESTERN ONTARIO.

THE CENTRAL BRANCH OF THE LONDON PUBLIC LIBRARY
MOVED TO IT'S NEW LOCATION IN 2002 ALONG DUNDAS STREET.
THIS OPEN CONCEPT "STATE OF THE ART" FACILITY
HAS OVER 275,000 BOOKS AND 41,000 AUDIO VISUAL ITEMS.

*Having been a resident of this great city for over forty years
and as Chief of Police, my love for the city grows stronger each year.
In addition to the aesthetic value of the Forest City captured in these
photographs, what makes the city so great is the people. London is a
very beautiful, safe, and caring community.*

Wm. Murray Faulkner
Chief of Police

COVENT GARDEN MARKET IS LOCATED ON THE ORIGINAL
HISTORIC MARKET SITE WHERE VENDORS HAVE BROUGHT GOODS
TO SELL FOR OVER 150 YEARS. FINE FOODS FROM AROUND THE WORLD
DRAW PEOPLE FROM ALL CORNERS OF THE CITY TO THE DOWNTOWN CORE
TO CELEBRATE THIS MAGNIFICENT COMMUNITY-FOCUSED FACILITY.

London's diverse architecture adds beauty
to the downtown core.

On Thursday and Saturday mornings
Covent Garden Market features a "farmers market".

Richard Bain's stunning photographs show you the beauty of our city from the wonderful array of people, to the breathtaking sights of our parks and many other notable places. As you tour London through these images I would like to say, "Welcome to my home".

Denise Pelley, Vocalist

THE "CASTLE" AT STORYBOOK GARDENS

IS THE ENTRANCE TO A MAGICAL EXPERIENCE

WHERE CHILDREN'S NURSERY RHYMES COME TO LIFE.

THE SPRINGBANK EXPRESS HAS BEEN
TRANSPORTING CHILDREN AND THEIR PARENTS
AROUND SPRINGBANK PARK SINCE 1958.

COOLING DOWN ON A SUMMER DAY AT THE IVEY PARK SPRAY PAD,
SITUATED AT THE FORKS OF THE THAMES.

A century old renovated "brownstone" along Princess Avenue.

SUNDAY MORNING IN VICTORIA PARK AMID THE AUTUMN COLOURS.

London showcases the diversity, creativity and energy of one of the finest cities in Canada. World class research, education, and health care, supporting strong, safe and vibrant neighbourhoods, a greener environment, beautiful parks and greenspaces, and an array of entertainment options like the John Labatt Centre – these are just a few of the things that define an exceptional city.

Anne Marie DeCicco-Best
Mayor, City of London

ALONG THE THAMES RIVER IN GIBBONS PARK.

MORNING MIST GREETS A CYCLIST ON THE GROUNDS OF ST. PETER'S SEMINARY.

CANOEISTS GLIDE ALONG THE THAMES IN A VEIL OF MIST.

WINTER AT GIBBONS PARK.

SPRINGBANK PARK AFTER AN EARLY WINTER SNOWFALL.

I have always found London a great city in which to walk. As a youngster my friends and I walked through the pleasant neighbourhoods of East London on our way to the Saturday matinee at the Odeon Theatre on Dundas Street. As a student at Western, I walked daily along Huron Street through the picturesque homes of North London on my way to classes. Today there is so much to see while on the way to concerts, restaurants or theatre. Victoria Park is alight in the winter and filled with sounds and aromas during the summer festivals… and I never tire of walking among the giant balloons and wicker baskets at the London Balloon Festival in Harris Park.

Jay Campbell, Meteorologist

ABOVE: HOT AIR BALLOON PILOTS RECEIVE
A WEATHER BRIEFING FROM METEOROLOGIST
JAY CAMPBELL PRIOR TO TAKING FLIGHT.

LEFT: READY TO LAUNCH AT THE
LONDON BALLOON FESTIVAL.

LIFT OFF FROM HARRIS PARK IS ALWAYS A THRILL
FOR THE THOUSANDS OF SPECTATORS WHO COME TO WATCH.

A winter's ice storm leaves the trees sparkling in
Victoria Park and on the grounds of St. Paul's Cathedral.

As the "People You Know" columnist for The London Free Press, I have had the good fortune to witness the generosity and kind spirit of Londoners. Day after day Londoners continue to give of themselves to help others, whether they are coaching a little league game, attending a fundraising dinner and auction or hitting the links for a charity golf tournament - Londoners never stop! To see this kindness first hand is inspiring.

Allison Graham
People You Know Columnist
The London Free Press

ENJOYING THE FOOD AT THE
FERRAGOSTO ITALIAN FESTIVAL IN FRONT
OF COVENT GARDEN MARKET.

A warm welcome always awaits you from Jack DiCarlo,
"Maitre d' Extraordinaire", at Michael's On The Thames.

FEEDING THE GEESE ALONG THE RIVER IN SPRINGBANK PARK.

Entertaining the crowds with food
and festivities at Rib-Fest.

TOP: SOME OF THE FINEST PREPARED CHICKEN AND CHIPS
BY RUI AT REI DOS LEITOES PORTUGUESE RESTAURANT ON HAMILTON ROAD.

BOTTOM: READY TO ENJOY A WRAP AT HOME COUNTY FOLK FESTIVAL.

A solitary hot air balloon greets the dawn over London's original Financial District on Ridout Street.

London offers all the opportunities of a much larger city while enjoying the cozy,
small town feeling that comes from having cornfields only 15 minutes from downtown.
We're known for the quality of our educational institutions, our health care and research facilities,
a thriving business community and an active cultural scene. What more could you want?

Denis Devos
President and Chief Operating Officer, London Life

Looking out over Victoria Park
is the stately offices of London Life
Insurance Company.

ABOVE: THE MIDDLESEX COUNTY BUILDING WAS BUILT
IN 1829 TO SERVE AS A COURTHOUSE AND COUNTY JAIL.

LEFT: THE DOMINION PUBLIC BUILDING ALONG
RICHMOND STREET AT DUSK.

The Royal Scots re-enact the Battle of Longwoods,
which took place along the Thames River near
Delaware in 1814.

The London Museum of Archaeology is the site
of Canada's only ongoing public excavation
of a 15th century Native village.

ABOVE: The Denfield General Store, built in 1877
is now part of Fanshawe Pioneer Village.
It was relocated to this living history site in 1997.

LEFT: Tending the springtime flowers at Eldon House,
London's oldest residence that was built in 1834
by Captain John Harris.

ORCHESTRA LONDON PROJECTS
AN ARTISTIC IMAGE TO THE COMMUNITY
THROUGH FINE MUSIC.

London has a remarkable diversity of cultural activities, ranging from the thousands of school children who participate annually in the Kiwanis Music Festival to world class guest artists who appear with our own Orchestra London, from professional live theatre presented in the nationally recognized and century old Grand Theatre to the many community based theatre groups. Londoners have available to them a broad range of festivals, multi-cultural events and visual arts presentations. My involvement with the board of Orchestras Canada has made me realize that London is very well regarded within the national arts community, certainly a city of which to be proud.

John Kennedy
Past President, Orchestra London

THE JEANS 'N CLASSICS BAND TAKES A BREAK
IN VICTORIA PARK BETWEEN REHEARSALS.

DANCING AND JAZZ AT COVENT GARDEN MARKET.

The old Talbot Inn streetscape
has been incorporated into
the John Labatt Centre.

Kingsmill's Ltd - A Landmark Specialty Department Store since 1865, is located in The Heart of London's Historic Business District. Six generations of the Kingsmill family have been proud to serve this beautiful and historic city. Time has brought many changes to the city's core, and we have watched them happen, as we still do today. One thing remains constant, and that is the loyalty and spirit of so many who continue to patronize this great part of our City.

Fred Kingsmill
Vice-President, Kingsmill's Ltd.

KINGSMILL'S DEPARTMENT STORE,
A DOWNTOWN LONDON LANDMARK.

ABOVE: ONE OF LONDON'S OLDEST BUSINESSES,
NASH JEWELLERS HAS BEEN FAMILY OWNED AND
OPERATED SINCE 1918.

RIGHT: NOVACKS HAS BEEN SERVING LONDON OUTDOOR
ENTHUSIASTS FROM ITS KING STREET LOCATION SINCE 1939.
IT IS DESERVEDLY KNOWN AS LONDON'S MOST INTERESTING STORE.

*It's a fabulous morning in downtown London.
I look out over Victoria Park and the stately London
Life building from my office on the 11th floor of
City Hall. The sun is shining brightly and reflecting
off the stain glass windows from the church adjacent
to the Park. The majestic Victorian homes that line
the nearby neighbourhood streets have slate roofs with
geometric designs which are gleaming in the light.
At the far reaches of my view are the Forks of the
Thames where the banks are straining to hold back
the swollen waters. The winter snows now have
disappeared, and the trees are ready to explode with
new foliage. The grass is turning green from recent
rains, and there is a 'jump' in everyone's step from
the crisp clean air as they march off to work.
London's heritage stretches out beneath me and its
growing legacy is visible in all directions from my
vantage point. Spring is just around the corner and
new life is emerging from under the snow as London
begins another year. The past has been generous to
this City and the future is as bright as the morning's
sunlight. I can't help but remind myself what a
special City we have and how fortunate I am
to live here.*

*Jeff Fielding
Chief Administrative Officer, City of London*

LOOKING OUT AT THE DOMINION PUBLIC
BUILDING AND THE TALBOT CENTRE FROM
THE GROUNDS OF ST. PAUL'S CATHEDRAL.

Flowers and food add to the flavour
of Richmond Row.

One London Place and St. Paul's Cathedral
reflected in the glass of the Talbot Centre.

London is a very special community characterized by many hectares of beautiful parklands and unique naturalized areas which feed both the eye and the soul. The City is distinguished by a blend of modern and traditional architecture that reflects a respect for the past and an embracement of the future. Our unique festivals, many attractions and spectacular events beckon visitors from all across Canada and the world to experience a community that loves to laugh and live.

John Winston
General Manager, Tourism London

DOWNTOWN LONDON AT DUSK.

Fun for all ages at the Western Fair,
an annual event held each September since 1867.

A PHOTO FINISH AT WESTERN FAIR RACEWAY.

AN OWNER AND DRIVER HEAD BACK TO THE STABLES
AFTER A VICTORY ON THE TRACK.

A MAGNOLIA TREE IN BLOOM
ON THE GROUNDS OF ELDON HOUSE.

A "SECRET GARDEN" ALONG RICHMOND STREET
NEAR THE UNIVERSITY GATES.

September and a return to class,
as students make their way across
University Hill.

The University of Western Ontario and the City of London enjoy a long and supportive relationship. For over a century, Western has been part of London. Many of our faculty, staff, students and alumni live and work in this community, contributing to its economy, its cultural and intellectual vibrancy, and its social diversity. Nearly every community group has among its leaders people who are affiliated with the University, and our stature as a national centre for education, health care and health research, and scientific discovery derives largely from the synergy of our University, research institutes, teaching hospitals, and a supportive community. Western is proud of our association with London and Southwestern Ontario and of the role we play in the life of this region.

Paul Davenport
President and Vice-Chancellor, The University of Western Ontario

THE WESTERN MUSTANGS CARRY THE BALL
FOR ANOTHER TOUCHDOWN AT
TD WATERHOUSE STADIUM.

A purple sky over University College.

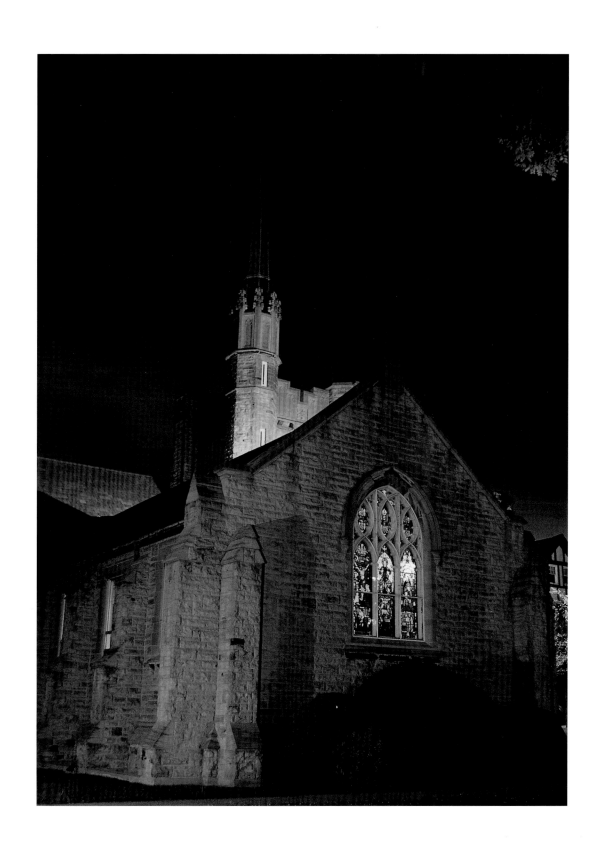

HURON UNIVERSITY COLLEGE, ESTABLISHED IN 1863,
IS THE FOUNDING COLLEGE AT WESTERN.

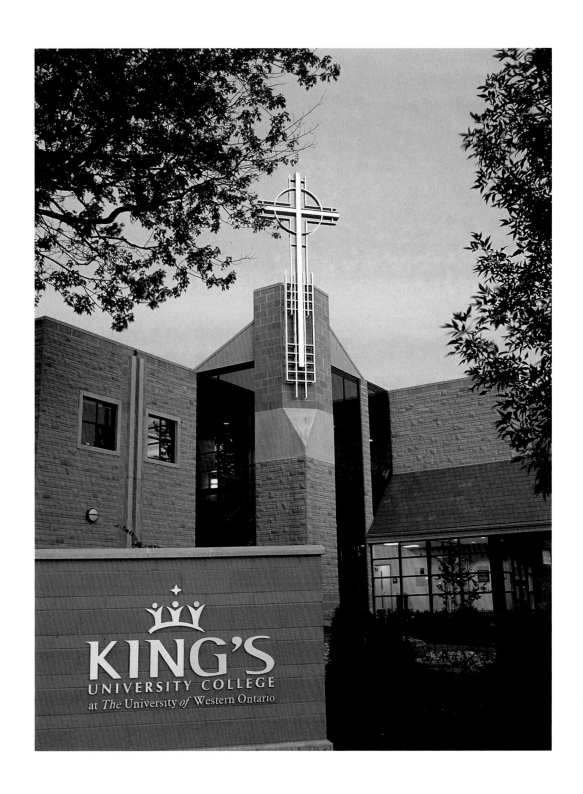

ABOVE: THE SETTING SUN ILLUMINATES
ELIZABETH A. "BESSIE" LABATT HALL
AT KING'S UNIVERSITY COLLEGE.

LEFT: THE TUNNEL SPANNING TALBOT COLLEGE
AND THE DON WRIGHT FACULTY OF MUSIC AT WESTERN.

Pete and I have been Londoners for more than 45 years, arriving here from Woodstock to attend Western. We never left! As a teacher, a citizenship judge, a University of Western Ontario board chair and now as CEO of London Community Foundation, I have been privileged to sample so many aspects of this beautiful city: the individuality of her neighbourhoods, restaurants and cafés, the richness and scope of her academic life, the incredible spirit of her volunteers and the diversity of her people who bring with them rich cultures from all parts of the world.

Libby Fowler
CEO, London Community Foundation

WATCHING THE ACTIVITY ALONG
RICHMOND STREET AT AN OUTDOOR CAFÉ.

ENJOYING A SUMMER NIGHT ON THE ROOFTOP PATIO
AT T. J. BAXTER'S ALONG RICHMOND ROW.

MERLA MAE IS A FAVORITE PLACE TO GO FOR ICE CREAM
ON A SUMMER EVENING.

Spring blossoms along Richmond Street.

A WINTER SNOWFALL BLANKETS THE TREES
ALONG ST. GEORGE STREET.

Two of "Old North's" magnificent homes in winter.

Warming up before taking to the stage
at Home County Folk Festival in Victoria Park.

Having recently re-located to Toronto, I have come to even more deeply appreciate the people, parks and places of London, which Richard has again so magically captured for all time in his photographs. In fact, I now refer to my weekend escapes home to London – as my getaway to the "cottage".

Gord Harris
Long-time London radio personality
Program Director of AM640 Toronto Radio

ENJOYING AN AMUSEMENT RIDE IN FRONT OF
THE BAND SHELL AT HOME COUNTY.

ENTERTAINMENT FOR ALL AGES AT HOME COUNTY FOLK FESTIVAL.

*Aside form the natural beauty of London
and its well deserved reputation as a great place
to live and work, I am increasingly impressed with
the zeal of the community and our collective will
to achieve – to do better. After having lived here
for just ten years I have witnessed a tremendous
spirit in London that really does transcend all
of the normal dividing lines. Business, sport,
academia, life sciences, volunteerism and yes, even
politics, has a different feel to it than any of the
dozen or more communities I have lived in. Anyone
who still holds the view that London is a tired old
conservative community that's unwilling to change
simply hasn't been here in the last decade.
I'm very proud of our community and what
we have been able to accomplish and to those
who haven't been here in a while – I invite
you to share in that pride.*

*Gerry Macartney
General Manager and C.E.O.
London Chamber of Commerce*

THE JOHN LABATT CENTRE IS HOME
TO THE LONDON KNIGHTS AS WELL AS
NUMEROUS CONCERTS AND EVENTS
THROUGHOUT THE YEAR. IT CONSISTENTLY
RANKS AS ONE OF THE MOST SUCCESSFUL
ENTERTAINMENT VENUES IN THE WORLD.

Dressed in "Green" to cheer on the hometown team.

ANOTHER GOAL FOR THE MEMORIAL CUP CHAMPIONS,
THE LONDON KNIGHTS.

Our city, with its beautiful parks and trails, the Thames, and an abundance
of year round activities brings great joy and pleasure to our residents including
those we serve who are considering locating a business here. London truly
is a great place to live, work and play.

John Kime
President & CEO, London Economic Development Corporation

DOWNTOWN LONDON'S DIVERSE
ARCHITECTURE AS SEEN FROM THE
WHARNCLIFFE ROAD BRIDGE.

THE NEWLY RENOVATED LONDON
INTERNATIONAL AIRPORT HAS RECEIVED A
RECENT ADDITION WITH THIS REFURBISHED
CT-33 TRAINER.

TOP: AT THE NEWS DESK AT FANSHAWE COLLEGE'S BROADCAST CENTER,
WHERE RADIO, TELEVISION AND BROADCAST JOURNALISM ARE TAUGHT.
BOTTOM: A STUDENT AT WORK ON A PROJECT IN A WELDING LAB.

LEFT: FANSHAWE COLLEGE HAS AN IMPRESSIVE ENROLLMENT
OF OVER 14,000 FULL TIME STUDENTS AND 20,000 PART TIME STUDENTS,
AND OFFERS OVER 100 POST SECONDARY SCHOOL COURSES TO MEET
THE GROWING NEEDS OF BUSINESS, INDUSTRY, HEALTHCARE AND
GOVERNMENT. THE STUDENT CENTRE AT FANSHAWE COLLEGE IS HOME
TO A VARIETY OF STUDENT-ORIENTATED FACILITIES AND SERVICES.

THE ROBARTS RESEARCH INSTITUTE,
ESTABLISHED IN 1986, FOCUSES ON
NEUROLOGICAL, CARDIOVASCULAR AND
IMMUNE-RELATED DISORDERS.

The people of London have access to one of the most innovative, high-quality healthcare networks in the country. The level of collaboration and integration that exists between London Health Sciences Centre and St. Josephs Health Care, has allowed us to enhance and build on our tertiary and acute care specialties, form one of Canada's most successful research partnerships, and play a key role in advancing the medical profession as teaching hospitals affiliated with the University of Western Ontario.

My dual role at London's hospitals has allowed me to see first hand how both organizations are taking on new roles and responsibilities as part of their commitment to providing the best care possible to our community and region.

Cliff Nordal
President and CEO,
London Health Sciences Centre
St. Joseph's Health Care, London

READY FOR TAKE-OFF FROM THE UNIVERSITY CAMPUS OF LONDON HEALTH SCIENCES CENTRE.

ABOVE: THE NATIONAL RESEARCH COUNCIL OF CANADA
IS HOME TO THE INTEGRATED MANUFACTURING TECHNOLOGIES INSTITUTE.

RIGHT: BUILT IN 1925 FOR THE SMALLMAN FAMILY,
WINDERMERE MANOR IS NOW A CONFERENCE CENTER, HOTEL
AND RESTAURANT LOCATED AT WESTERN'S RESEARCH PARK.

It was The University of Western Ontario that brought me here in the early '70s, but it is the people; the elegance of our city and Victoria Park's squirrels that keep me here. London is a city that lets you get involved – just miss a meeting and you will find out just how much.

Think about this… in one city, where else can you go and find the best education system, from elementary to post-secondary… the best hospitals with facilities that are second to none! And the arts… from the Grand to the Orchestra; from youth drama to kids' sports… London has it all.

The farthest point from anywhere in London to downtown is 15 minutes and rush hour is 8 cars in a row. Ours is a big city with small town values – how amazing is that!

Edwin A. Holder
President
Stevenson & Hunt Insurance Brokers Limited

LONDON'S EXTENSIVE TRAILS LOCATED PRIMARILY ALONG THE THAMES MAKES FOR SOME EXCELLENT CYCLING.

A MORNING WALK THROUGH GREENWAY PARK.

ENJOYING A ROUND OF GOLF
AT THE LONDON HUNT & COUNTRY CLUB.

Competing in the club championships
at the London Ski Club, Boler Mountain.

ON THE WAY TO THE RINK FOR A FAMILY SKATE...
AND ENJOYING THE HOLIDAY LIGHTS AT VICTORIA PARK.

There is an old rock'n'roll ballad from the fifties with the title "You don't know what you've got until you lose it". When I moved away from London in 1979 I enjoyed where I lived but every time we came back to visit friends in the Forest City, it felt like we were coming home. Home is where your heart is, where your friends are, where you're most comfortable. So, the next time I'm stuck in a construction zone behind six hundred cars I will keep reminding myself... "I'm home, I'm home, I'm home".

Joe Duchesne
Morning Show Host, AM 980

COMPETING IN THE GUS MACKER 3-ON-3
BASKETBALL TOURNAMENT IN DOWNTOWN LONDON.

THE ICE HOUSE IS NOW HOME TO THE FOREST CITY VELODROME
FOR INDOOR BICYCLE RACING ENTHUSIASTS. FORMERLY KNOWN AS
TREASURE ISLAND GARDENS, THE ROLLING STONES PLAYED
HERE IN 1965 AND JOHNNY CASH PROPOSED TO JUNE CARTER
DURING A CONCERT ON FEBRUARY 22ND, 1968.

MEMBERS OF THE LONDON CANOE CLUB GATHER
AFTER AN EVENING ON THE WATER.

An early morning rowing practice on Fanshawe Lake.

Winter blows its strength.
London's washed with white; but,
Spring's relief is nie.

Spring's beauty ripens!
London seldom seems so fine.
Greenish hues abound.

Mid-August's balloons
Cram our blue skies with color.
We can't wait for Fall.

Can London's Autumns
Be ever matched? – no way!
We have it all here.

London, my home town
But, room to be home for more.
There's a place for us!

Anthony Little, Lawyer
Little & Jarrett

Enjoying a walk amid the fall colours
in the Rayner Rose Garden.

ABOVE: OFF FOR A HIKE IN THE MEDWAY VALLEY.

LEFT: SPENDING TIME ALONG THE BANKS
OF THE THAMES RIVER.

ABOVE: Young naturalists looking for crayfish
along Medway Creek in London.

RIGHT: Some early morning fishing enthusiasts get
ready for a big catch at Fanshawe Lake.

ACKNOWLEDGEMENTS

When I decided to bring out this third volume of photographs, celebrating London, I wanted to capture some of the "people, parks and places" that make our city such a special place. There really is something magical about watching hot air balloons lift off on a summer evening from Harris Park... heading over to Victoria Park to sample the fare at Rib-Fest... then enjoying a glass of wine in a jazz club along Richmond Row. London is a remarkable place!

It was an honour to have Victor Garber agree to write a personal foreword for this book. Mr. Garber's fond memories of London are evidenced in his written reflections. It always amazes me that individuals as busy as he, in a chosen career, still find time to give back to a place that means so much to them. Victor is truly a generous man, and London should be proud of his contributions to both our city and the world stage.

Thanks to Anne Marie DeCicco-Best, Jay Campbell, Paul Davenport, Denis Devos, Joe Duchesne, Murray Faulkner, Jeff Feilding, Libby Fowler, Allison Graham, Gord Harris, Deb Harvey, Edwin Holder, John Kennedy, Fred Kingsmill, John Kime, Anthony Little, Gerry Macartney, Cliff Nordal, Denise Pelley and John Winston for their ongoing contributions to London and to this book.

I would like to say a special thanks to Bill Brady, who has been an endless source of encouragement and humour. He is always willing to contribute not only to my work, but also endlessly to making this city a caring community.

It is amazing how a designer can take a group of images and produce a finished work. Peter Watson, Brian Ripley, Amanda Jean Francis and Michelle Hart from Response Generators did just that, and I appreciate their patience in accommodating all of the changes that a photographer can throw their way. Thanks also to Tom Klassen from Friesens Book Division who was instrumental in the production.

I extend heartfelt thanks to my wife Joan, who always finds the time to look at my images at the end of a shoot, and to our four children, Caroline, Daniel, Brett and Jordan. Each of you in your own way have been tremendously supportive, and I hope that as life takes you to other places, you always treasure your time spent here.

Finally, to all who love London, and to all who live here, may this collection of photographs remind you of the "people, parks and places" that make this city such a remarkable place.

Richard Bain